RISK TAKER

HOW GOD SPEAKS

JAMIE URICK

Warrior House LLC
Jamie@WarriorHouseLLC.com

Copyright © 2022 by Jamie Urick.

All rights reserved. No part of this book may be reproduced or transmitted in any form or by any means, electronic, or mechanical, including photocopying, recording, or by any information storage and retrieval system, without written permission from the author, except for the inclusion of brief quotations for a review, without the prior permission of the publisher.

Published by Warrior House LLC
P.O. Box 871
Frankfort, Illinois 60423 USA
Contact author: Jamie@WarriorHouseLLC.com

All Scripture quotations are taken from the New International Version of the Bible unless otherwise noted.
**THE HOLY BIBLE, NEW INTERNATIONAL VERSION ®, NIV ® COPYRIGHT © 1973, 1978, 1984, 2011 by Biblica, Inc. ® Used by permission.
All rights reserved worldwide.**

ISBN: 979-8-9868108-0-5 (Paperback)

Cover Design by: alex_studio698 Fiverr

Printed in the United States of America.

*I dedicate this book to my loving husband,
Michael R. Urick.*

Contents

Introduction i

To The Reader iii

1. The Tractor 1

2. The Semi Truck 17

3. The Tie Rod 23

4. Revelations from God... 39

5. There's More!... 51

6. Conclusion.. 59

7. Buyer's Remorse 63

8. The Gospel.. 65

9. Where to Start.. 71

Introduction

I'M TAKING A risk sharing my faith and sharing how God spoke to me. But He's worth the risk. I am a *Risk Taker*.

By God's grace and mercy, He has saved my life from certain death many times. I have chosen three of those times to share with you today to show you how God speaks, how He warns, and how He prepares us for what's ahead.

> *"I will tell of the kindnesses of the Lord,*
> *the deeds for which he is to be praised,*
> *according to all the Lord has done for us..."*
> Isaiah 63:7

This is a true story. No events have been changed or altered.

To The Reader

THERE IS ONE message in this book: **You can hear God's voice**. He speaks through His Word, through His Creation, and He speaks personally to your heart as you will see in this book.

When I was at my lowest, I prayed this verse over and over and over again: *"I will not die but live, and will proclaim what the Lord has done."* Psalm 118:17

I did not die, I did live, and I am proclaiming what the LORD has done for me so that you will know and experience His loving voice personally too.

So, *"Come and hear, all you who fear God; let me tell you what he has done for me"* Psalm 66:16. Because **He will do it for you.**

CHAPTER ONE
The Tractor

*"Call to Me and I will answer you,
and show you great and mighty things,
which you do not know."*
Jeremiah 33:3 KJV

IT HAD BEEN a long and bitter Chicago winter. The pewter skies gave way to a stunning robin's egg blue hue. My husband Mike and I were just finishing building a house in a new subdivision that used to be a farmer's field. The electric company trenched a three-foot-deep line from the corner of the property where the electric is located, and also where the phone pedestal is located, to the house to run electricity. The trench line was a visible scar that ran diagonally across the lawn. We moved in soon after on May 1st, 2001 and looked forward to our new adventure.

We had an old John Deere tractor that I used to mow the lawn every week the rest of the spring, all summer, and all fall. The next spring it was time to mow again. I got on the

RISK TAKER

tractor as usual and started to mow around the perimeter of the property and then I would mow area by area like I did last year. As I was mowing the perimeter working my way east toward the electrical/telephone pedestal in the southeast corner of the property I heard an angel declare: "Do not go near the trench line or you will surely die!" I looked up and I saw angels, more angels than I could count. They were standing at the property line near the pedestal. They were several angels deep. They were taller than I would have imagined and their clothes were brilliant white and were translucent. They had swords but they were sheathed. One angel spoke for all.

I was not accustomed to hearing from angels, but it was undeniable. I got it! I believed it and I acted on it. I immediately turned the mower around and headed back to where I came from. I decided it was safe to mow the rest of the lawn, just not near the trench line so I kept mowing.

As I mowed the rest of the lawn, I wondered how I could surely die. I had mowed over that trench line last spring, all last summer, and all last fall. It looked the same. There were no trees or bushes to obscure my view; it still was just patches of grass and weeds. I didn't see anything disturbed, I didn't see anything different, but I believed the angel. I did not go near the trench line.

I mowed everything else I could mow and I went back, still keeping my distance from the trench line. Then I saw the army of angels again standing in a line, white, glistening, powerful, brilliant, and one spoke again for all. He said the same thing: "Do not go near the trench line or you will surely die!"

I turned around again and went back to the garage. I left the tractor outside in the driveway and went in the house to wait for Mike to come home. I was not going near that trench line again.

Mike came home. I told him what happened. I knew that he trusted me, but I also knew how strange my words sounded. "Hey honey, I heard from an angel that if I went near the trench line I would surely die."

But, I know that I heard from the angel, he did not. I had to make him understand. I had to make him get it. In order to emphasize how serious this situation was I literally grabbed hold of his jacket on each side of the zipper and with a little tug I said: "Believe me. If you go near the trench line you will surely die." I was not hysterical, I was serious. I was dead serious. He needed to hear me, he needed to believe me. His life depended on it. He said almost word for word what I had thought: "But, we mowed it all last year. Nothing has been disturbed. What could go wrong? What could possibly be dangerous enough to cause you or me to die?" I said "I don't know, I am telling you what I know, and that is what the angel said: 'You will surely die.'"

RISK TAKER

Mike went outside and got on the tractor and drove near the trench line. Apparently, no angel spoke to him. I called a friend for prayer on my cell phone and on the house phone I dialed 91 ready to push the other 1 for emergency help. I was prepared.

He started near the phone pedestal and mowed toward the house. He mowed parallel with the trench line but not on the trench line. He was going so slowly, then I saw him turn off the tractor, get off the tractor, lay down on the ground on his stomach, perpendicular to the trench line. Something caught his attention. He started pulling hunks of dirt, mud, and grass away from this one spot. I knew he was strong but how could he pull hunks of dirt so easily?

I was concerned, my heart was pounding. Then, Mike got up and walked in the house. I told my friend I'd call her back and I hung up. I also hung up the other phone that was ready to finish dialing 911. He came in and said "How did you know?"

"Know what?" I asked.

He asked again, "How did you know?"

Again, I said "Know what? I don't know anything. I told you everything I know. What is it?"

He said, "There is a sink hole. It is a large sink hole."

JAMIE URICK

When the electric company trenched the line, they cut through a field tile. A field tile is not like a flat floor tile; it is a pipe made of clay that farmers bury to divert water to prevent flooding. Because they are made of clay, they do not show up on detection devices that are used before digging or trenching. So, it is vital that when you dig or trench that you watch carefully for evidence of a broken tile. It is made of clay so it is easy to see shards of clay when trenching or digging when you cut through it. If you cut through the pipe it has to be repaired or you will flood.

In this case, the electric company trenched the line, cutting through the buried clay pipe (tile) and did not repair it nor report it. That means last spring, all last summer, all last fall, and all last winter water was going through the pipe and pooling, then going out the other end of the broken pipe taking with it dirt creating a sink hole. Week after week it was wearing away the soil until only a thin layer of top soil and grass remained.

The angel was warning me of the sink hole! If I or Mike, or anyone would have walked over it, let alone mowed over it, we would have fallen in.

Mike could not believe that there was actually something wrong. We had seen nothing. We knew nothing, but I believed and acted on what the angel said and Mike acted on what I said, even if he didn't completely believe me. I was praising God with a strength and fullness of heart I

RISK TAKER

didn't know I had. My husband also praised God but he still didn't understand how I could have known. I kept telling him, I didn't know, the angel told me. It was from God! He saved our lives!

I called my friend and told her what we found and she was amazed. Together we praised God! How good, how gracious, how amazing for Him to send angels to warn me - not once but twice. And, I was so grateful that I believed it and acted upon it. And, I was not embarrassed or timid; I did not care how I looked to my husband because I was certain what I heard. I did not care how it sounded or what he, or my friend, thought of me. I loved him enough to warn him. I loved him enough to grab hold of his jacket to emphasize the seriousness of this situation. I loved him enough to risk looking like a fool in order to warn him. I did not look at the natural, I did not dismiss what I heard, and I acted on it. And, we are alive because of it.

I was praising God all day. He loved me enough to warn me and I exercised my faith to believe it and to warn Mike.

Then, that night, lying in bed I recounted everything and found a problem. The sink hole was only 3-4 feet deep. How could we have surely died? "Surely died" means not just a chance we would have died, we would have surely, certainly, 100%, without a doubt died. How could that be? I asked God. I said "Lord, I come before you humbly, and I truly believe the Word that was spoken that we would have surely died, but I don't understand how. Please do not be harsh with me, I just don't understand. I believe but I don't see. I don't understand. The hole was just 3-4 feet deep. There was water, about a foot deep but I could not have drowned in it. If the tractor went over the sink hole at any angle it would tip or fall just 3-4 feet. I could walk or crawl out. What am I missing Lord?"

I didn't have to wait long. He said: "The blades were engaged." I stopped breathing right then and there. He unveiled Truth to my mind and I saw it. There are three blades on this tractor, and when the blades are engaged it means they are spinning. This tractor has a five-foot cutting width and the three blades covering the entire underbelly of the tractor. If it had tipped or fallen in at any angle the spinning blades would have cut through the electrical line and I, or Mike, would have been electrocuted instantly because of the water in the sink hole.

I could not breathe. It's true! I would **have** surely died. Mike would **have** surely died. I see it! I see it completely! God saved our lives from certain death. I praised Him most of the night. I didn't want to go to sleep. I wanted to thank and praise Him.

The next morning, I could not wait to tell Mike what God had revealed to me. I walked him through my prayer, withholding God's response. He agreed with my assessment,

RISK TAKER

he also did not understand how we would have surely died; it was just a 3-4-foot-deep hole.

Then I told him what God said: "The blades were engaged." I did not have to say another word, his face said it all. He pieced it together in an instant. He said, "Jamie! The blades were engaged! The blades would have cut through the electrical line and you would have been electrocuted!"

I said "Yes, I know!" Then I added, "There was water in the hole too."

He said "YES!!! There was water too! Water, electric, blades, metal tractor…" his voice tailed off as he was deep in thought.

Then he said, as if correcting me, "You don't understand, you would have DIED!" I said, "I know! That's what I've been telling you."

We were both blown away at this revelation. We thanked and praised God, and I thanked Mike for believing me. He said "But, I didn't believe you. I couldn't see it, but I know your character and I had to check it out."

I knew he didn't believe me. That's why I was persistent. He didn't believe me because he didn't hear it from the angel, I heard it. It was my job to convince him. It was my job to keep him safe. I had to be as convincing to Mike as the angels were to me.

God warned me through an angel. God warned Mike through me.

APPLY IT

How has God sent a warning to you?

_____

_____

_____

_____

_____

_____

_____

_____

APPLY IT

How did you exercise your faith to believe it?

_____

_____

_____

_____

_____

_____

_____

_____

RISK TAKER

APPLY IT

How did you risk looking like a fool to warn others?

_____

_____

_____

_____

_____

_____

_____

_____

APPLY IT

Did you love others enough to warn them or did you keep it to yourself?

_____

_____

_____

_____

_____

_____

_____

APPLY IT

Starting today, when God sends you a warning will you exercise your faith to believe it and act on it?

_____

_____

_____

_____

_____

_____

_____

APPLY IT

Do you believe that you can go to God with your doubts and questions? How have you taken your doubts and questions to God?

_____

_____

_____

_____

_____

_____

_____

RISK TAKER

APPLY IT

Know today that God warns. Know today that He is approachable, loving, and quick to respond. Know today that He still speaks. What can you learn about God and your walk with Him from this story? How will it change your life?

_____

_____

_____

_____

_____

_____

CHAPTER TWO
The Semi Truck

"For God does not show favoritism."
Romans 2:11

THIS VERSE MEANS that what God did for one He will do for another.

I was a leader in Bible Study Fellowship (BSF) and I was on my way to Leader's Meeting one beautiful Tuesday morning. I pulled out of my driveway and drove down the street to the two-way stop sign. We live in a rural area, not much traffic. I was barely on time and needed to get going.

The intersection is simple. I'm stopped at the stop sign. There is a stop sign on the opposite side of the road and there was no oncoming traffic as far as I could see. I was going to make a left turn onto Center Road which is a single lane in each direction, with a speed limit of 55 mph. I looked to my right, no traffic. I looked to my left and I saw a semi-truck

RISK TAKER

approaching me from the north heading south. I had plenty of time to turn left in front of the semi and continue on my way in the single lane going north.

Then, I heard a still small voice say "wait." It was not even "Wait" with a capital W. It was "wait." It had a period after the word. It was a complete sentence. It was spoken with such gentleness yet authority. I heard it just once. I looked again. I had plenty of time to go. There was just this one semi. There was no reason to wait. But…I waited.

I said to myself, "I could have gone." "I could have gone again." "I could still make it." "I have to get to BSF." But again, I chose to wait. I would wait until the semi passed.

As it got closer, then I saw it. As the semi was approaching on my left, I saw an SUV passing it. If I had gone, I would have had a head-on collision with an SUV. He was going at least 55 mph to pass the semi. The semi did not alert me that there was an SUV passing him. I could not see the SUV because under the semi trailer there was a plastic trailer skirt that prevented me from seeing a vehicle driving next to him. And, the SUV was passing in a no passing zone. There was no way for me to have known that there was an SUV in the lane that I would be turning on to. And, I was driving an escort station wagon. Not much protection against an SUV going at least 55 mph. I would have surely died.

JAMIE URICK

God saved my life again. He said "wait." I saw no reason to wait, but I waited, and He saved my life.

Thank you, Lord!!!

That night I prayed and I thanked God for hours for saving my life. I was so grateful that I waited even though I saw no reason to wait. Then He said, "You hear My voice." I said "Yes!" but I didn't understand the fullness of what He meant. I was just filled with praise and thanksgiving and wonder that He saved my life, again.

APPLY IT

When have you heard a still small voice?

_____

_____

_____

_____

_____

_____

_____

_____

APPLY IT

Will you share your story with someone else, to encourage them?

_____

_____

_____

_____

_____

_____

_____

RISK TAKER

APPLY IT

Will you ask God to give you ears to hear and eyes to see? Your life may depend on it.

CHAPTER THREE
The Tie Rod

*"See, I have engraved you on the palms of my hands;
your walls are ever before me."*
Isaiah 49:16

I WORKED FOR a stockbroker for several years and I loved every minute of it. My husband and I were scheduled to go on a cruise to celebrate our wedding anniversary in just a few days and to prepare we were going to meet after work at a department store to look for a few dress shirts for him for the trip. Mike works in construction and his days are long and varied. As a result, we never meet somewhere after work. Never. I worked off of Route 30 and we were going to meet a couple miles down Route 30 at a department store at 5:30 p.m.

We have an account with my boss' company that we had saved money, bit by bit, dollar by dollar, for years. It was for a new car for me. My Escort Wagon – yes, I was still driving the same car - was fifteen years old. The account had more than enough for a new car for me. About a year ago I felt like we should not invest this money, that we should keep it in cash. Mike agreed, so it sat in a money market account, not invested. That was unlike me. If we had money it was going to work for us. To have that amount of money in cash, earning nothing, never happened before. I couldn't explain it; I just felt that's what we were supposed to do so we did it.

Then, the afternoon I was to meet Mike at a department store, I felt the Holy Spirit prompt me to do something. It literally felt like a tap on my right shoulder. I immediately got up, walked into my boss' office and said, "I don't know why, but I feel the Holy Spirit prompting me to transfer the money out of this account and into our personal checking account. I don't know why or for what reason, I just know that we are going to need that money. I wanted to let you know that I'm going to wire all the money from this account to our checking account today and close the account." He was a man of God and simply said "Ok."

I went back to my desk and, without hesitation or delay, wired it all to our checking account and closed the account.

This was huge for me for many reasons. First, we are savers; we don't withdrawal money that is earmarked for a specific purpose unless we use it for that purpose. Second, I didn't know why I had to take the money out, I just felt like the Holy Spirit prompted me to. Third, I paid for it to be wired to our checking account. It was $15. The amount is not the problem; the point is I never pay fees. I plan ahead so I avoid paying fees. But I knew it had to be done today so I paid the wire fee. I knew I could not wait for a check to be printed and mailed and then taken to the bank to be deposited even though that was just a couple days away. I had to wire the money today. And, lastly, I closed the account. I don't close accounts. Somehow, I knew that this account would not be funded again with this money or other money for quite some time. I was right.

I was on my way to meet Mike; I was driving about 30 mph and then Bam! My front tie rod broke on the right side. It doesn't sound like much, but when a tie rod brakes, the vehicle, and you inside the vehicle, immediately stops. Immediately. It's like hitting a wall at 30 mph but there is no wall. Even at 30 mph that's a huge unexpected impact. I felt ok but rattled. I immediately called Mike, he was already in the department store's parking lot, so he got on the road to meet me just a few minutes later.

The car was towed to our mechanic's garage and Mike and I drove home.

We were praising God!! If I were not meeting Mike that evening, I would have driven home my regular route which were rural back roads going 55 mph. If the tie rod would have broken at 55 mph it is safe to say, my Escort Station

RISK TAKER

Wagon would have flipped on the road or into a ditch killing me. God saved my life again.

I could not believe that I was unharmed. And, I thought the money must have been needed to pay for the car repairs, but I doubted that was it since the amount of money was more than enough to buy a new vehicle, not just to cover a repair.

Then, two days later, I was lifting something and I felt something in my neck give way. The pain got worse and worse as the day progressed. To make a long story short my countenance was frozen, my pain was a blinding nine on a scale of one to ten. I could not speak. I could barely open my mouth. I had severe lung spasms day and night. Lung spasms were like getting the wind knocked out of you, and it happened hundreds of times a day. I had constant dreams that someone was attacking me with an ax to my head. If I just touched my face I began to lose consciousness. I could not work. Doctors could find no answers. MRIs, CT scans, nothing. I threw up pain medications. Doctor after doctor, specialist after specialist, test after test, and no one could figure out what was wrong. I was bed ridden, imprisoned in extreme pain. Thanksgiving came and went. Our cruise came and went. Our wedding anniversary came and went. Christmas came and went. I could not speak a single word; I could not move my eyes. I had to write everything to communicate and many times I was too weak to hold a pen.

JAMIE URICK

One day I wrote: "My car broke and then I broke." I was trying to communicate that I was not sick, I was injured. Doctors dismissed it. New Year's holiday came and went. Three long months went by. My body was weak and breaking down. I still could not speak. I still could not work. Thankfully the doctor found a pain reliever that I didn't throw up and it reduced my pain down to a seven. Still unbelievable pain, but what a relief it was to have pain a seven and not a nine. That was grace. That was mercy.

I chose to praise God in my head. There were months where all I could think and focus on was "Jesus". It was just that one word. Just that one Name kept me going. It is the Name above every Name. I could not even think of an entire sentence the pain was so bad. Just "Jesus" and I knew that was enough.

I could praise Him because He gave me such a gift. Remember the Holy Spirit prompted me to transfer that money to our checking account? That's what we needed to pay our bills, to pay for doctor co pays, to pay for my car to be repaired, and to have margin so there were no financial worries while we were in this battle. Every bill was on auto pay, so during this horrific time, every bill was paid in full and on time. That alone told me that He knew this was coming. This assured me that it was going to be ok. That this is going to take awhile but that I am in His hands. He's got this. I'm ok. I'm going to be ok. That kept me going. That kept my spirits up. I kept reminding my heart of that. I kept stirring my faith with that one truth, that God saw this coming and He prepared us for it.

Remember, the very afternoon of my accident the Holy Spirit prompted me to transfer all the money into our checking account. If I had waited even one day, I couldn't have done it. If I had ignored it, I would not have that assurance to hold on to during those dark months. And, because of the prompting of the Holy Spirit a year before to keep the money out of investments we had that money in cash ready to be transferred. If it were invested, we would have had to wait three business days until the trades settled and then transfer it. We didn't have days. The accident was in just a few hours.

We didn't get to take that vacation on the cruise ship. It was our first two-week vacation ever. We didn't have a honeymoon because we couldn't afford it and we had decided before we got married that we would not start our marriage deeper in debt. We both had debt, but our wedding could not put us deeper in debt. We could pay for our small wedding that just included immediate family but a honeymoon was out of the question. We got married on a Saturday and went back to work the following Tuesday. We had been married 22 years and we had taken just one other cruise for a week and loved it. We could not wait to go on another cruise. And this cruise was two whole weeks, with a balcony, to the Caribbean in December. That was unprecedented for us. It was a dream come true. We could afford it because we saved for years and the cruise line had a great sale. We were so looking forward to it. But we couldn't go. I was sidelined. But, how gracious of God! That meant that Mike was home with me for two whole weeks! That has never happened before. God was making a way.

After three months of constant, relentless pain, I wrote a note to my husband on a Kleenex box – at this point we had run out of paper in the house for me to write on. I wrote that my body is breaking down and regardless of what is going on I need physical therapy. He contacted our Chiropractor and he referred us to Dustin. Any movement made me nauseous and it was a long drive, but he came highly recommended so we brought a bucket and we went.

Mike held the door to the physical therapy office as I ever-so-slowly hobbled in. As each person saw me, they froze. The receptionist, the patients, and even the physical therapists froze. I was that bad. In the exam room he said "I know exactly what's wrong with you. You have whiplash. But you have whiplash in the front, not in the back. That's why you can't speak, you can't open your mouth, you can't move your eyes, and you can't move your head. That's why you have lung spasms." Then he said, "You are so severe I'm not even going to touch you today. But I'm going to show you one technique that you can do on yourself and you will see improvement within two days. The improvement you will see is confirmation that it is whiplash. Then, come back to me in three days." He continued, "I have another woman with the same issue. This is fixable. You will be fine." I cried. When your countenance is frozen there is no contortion of your face, just a flood of tears cascading down your face and the pain spikes.

I knew my problem was simple! I knew it was fixable. Everyone tried to make it difficult and complex but it was simple - it was whiplash.

He showed me the technique on himself and he watched as I copied his movements on my neck. When he saw I was doing it exactly as he instructed, he nodded his head in approval. Then I wrote "How often can I do this?" He said "As much as you want as long as you don't cause more pain."

I cried again. For the first time since my accident, I had an answer. That answer broke through all the confusion. That answer turned the tide in my suffering. That answer was the key to setting me free from the trauma of constant pain and a bedridden life. That answer felt like the very hand of God reaching down and choosing this moment to bring healing. With healing He was giving me mercy, understanding, and love that I desperately needed. What a joyous moment! Nothing had changed, yet everything had changed. I was still locked up, I still needed a bucket in my lap in case I got sick from the movement of the vehicle, but I finally, finally, finally had a diagnosis and a solution. Healing had begun.

JAMIE URICK

Most whiplashes happen when you are rear ended. I was not rear ended. My trauma came from the front of the car when the tie rod broke, then it was triggered when I lifted something a few days later. That's why no one saw it. Not the brain specialist, not the neurologist, not the DO, not the MD, not the ENT, not the Chiropractor. It was whiplash but it was in the front, not the back, manifesting in a frozen countenance and sever lung spasms. It was a physical therapist, who didn't look old enough to shave, to see me and immediately know what was wrong and how to fix it.

Praise the Lord!

We drove home and the tears flowed from my frozen face as I was praising God on the inside. I did those exercises every few minutes on my neck. Two days later I whispered to Mike my first words in over three months: "hi". He cried. I cried. Healing has begun. My body was so locked up that it took over nine months of physical therapy to work up to rubber bands. I remember when I could finally turn my head, I would just look at Mike sitting in his chair. He felt uncomfortable and I just could not help myself. For all these months I could not see his handsome, loving face unless it was directly in front of my eyes. It was a joy to be able to turn and to look at him. To describe everything Mike did for me, how he stood by me, how he encouraged me, and the suffering he endured would fill volumes of books. I am so proud of him and I would not have made it through without Mike. He is my hero. It took another two years for the lung spasms to subside. And it took another couple of months after that for the excruciating headaches to stop. I don't know how long it took, well over a year and a half, where I had the strength – without hurting myself – to take a pair of wet jeans from the washer and put into the dryer. I could put the jeans in the washer, carefully, one by one, to be washed, and I could take them out of the dryer carefully, one by one, but for well over a year and a half I could not take them from the washer to the dryer because they were too heavy and I would hurt my neck again. I was that fragile. It was a good ten years before I could be hugged by anyone other than Mike because it caused so much pain. I was that broken.

There are two reasons why it took so long for me to recover. First, it took three long months to diagnose whiplash. Because of that, I was really locked up and I had a lot of muscle loss. Second, I could only go to physical therapy twice a week because I could not drive myself. Then, when I was a bit better I went back to work. I worked three days a week. Looking back I went back too soon. I wanted to go back to work and I did not inquire of the Lord. That was wrong. I could barely whisper, and heaven help me if someone asked me to repeat something. I had to muster everything I had just to say something the first time, let alone repeat it. I quickly learned to knock on a table to get someone's attention at work or at home. When I had full eye contact, I would begin speaking/whispering. I had chosen every word carefully in order to speak as few words as possible. After I returned to work, I went to physical therapy one day a week. My recovery would have been much faster if I would have gone more often, but I am so grateful for what I had and the progress I was making.

At my worst, I could only focus on One Name: "Jesus". I would meditate on that Name over and over and over again. I would praise His Name in my head and in my heart. The pain was so great that I couldn't even focus on "Jesus Christ". Two words were too long. In time, the partial Bible verse that came to mind was: *"...sacrifice of praise..."* (Hebrews 13:15). I learned through this that when I am suffering, and when I choose to praise God for Who He is, that is a *sacrifice* of praise. The entire verse is:

"Through Jesus, therefore, let us continually offer to God a sacrifice of praise-the fruit of lips that openly profess His name" Hebrews 13:15.

I could praise God because I kept my eyes on Him. I kept encouraging my heart with the knowledge that He went before me. That He always goes before me. That He is always with me. That He's got this and that I can trust His character. He is Good. I didn't have to figure it all out. I didn't have to fix it. I just had to trust Him. God is never late. That focus gave me such deep gratitude that produced a sacrifice of praise. It was not praise under duress. It was praise from a deep gratitude that God is Good. The Bible tells us in Psalm 34:3 KJV *"O magnify the Lord with me, and let us exalt his name together!"* To magnify is to focus on something that looks small or that looks far away and magnify it until it becomes large in our eyes. When we do that, we see things in great detail that we would have missed. The same is true when we magnify God. We are able to see Him in great detail and then we know, we really know that God is bigger than our circumstances.

You can do the same.

God, in His mercy, healed me. I know that many are not healed. I don't have all the answers this side of heaven. But, when we trust in His character, we can rest in Him.

APPLY IT

God prepares His people. How has God prepared you for tough times?

_____

_____

_____

_____

_____

_____

_____

APPLY IT

Will you choose to stand on what He has revealed to you and praise Him?

_____

_____

_____

_____

_____

_____

_____

APPLY IT

How will you give God a sacrifice of praise today? We are not thanking Him for trouble; we are thanking Him for Who He is in the midst of trouble.

_____

_____

_____

_____

_____

_____

_____

RISK TAKER

APPLY IT

How will you magnify His Name and find rest in Him?

_____

_____

_____

_____

_____

_____

_____

_____

CHAPTER FOUR
Revelations from God

*"I have much more to say to you,
more than you can now bear."*
John 16:12

THREE TIMES GOD saved my life: The tractor, the semi truck, and the tie-rod breaking. But there's more. With God, there's always more. I invite you to walk with me through the revelations that God has given me since these events. He has a wonderful way of revealing a truth that is so powerful that it has to be revealed in parts because it's more than we can bear if it were all at once. Allow me to share with you these revelations so that you can know God better.

In bed, in the middle of the night, I would replay these three events over and over in my mind because I had a question for God. I felt like I was missing something. I knew that it was an angel that warned me by declaring "Do not go near the trench line or you will surely die!" I knew that it was the Holy Spirit who prompted me to transfer the money hours before the tie rod broke. But the voice that said "wait." was different. I could not put my finger on it. I knew it was from God but it was different. I had not heard it before. I was confused. I told people my story and I asked them why it was different and they didn't have an answer for me. I spent months pondering this, praying about it, asking the Lord: What am I missing?

Then, one night, He woke me up and replayed those events over and over again in my mind. I loved recounting it but I still felt like something was missing. I prayed and I thanked God for hours for saving my life. I was so grateful that I waited when I heard "wait." even though I saw no reason to wait. Then He said again what He said that night, "You hear My voice." I said again "Yes!" But He knew I didn't get it. He connected the dots for me the way only He could. He said "You hear *My* voice." Suddenly the answer was unveiled. He revealed to me "My" is "The Shepherd". He said: "You hear The Shepherd's voice." The Shepherd is Jesus! It was Jesus! It was Jesus' voice! It was Jesus' voice that spoke to me! The very Son of God! The creator of the Universe! That is why the voice was different. It was not the declaration of an angel, it was not the prompting of the Holy Spirit, it was the living God Himself who chose to speak to me. Me! That explains why it was a still small voice. Of course! How could I be so blind? That's why it was "wait." with a small "w" and a period. It had authority that only a King would have. It was not a declaration, it was not a prompt, it was a word. John 1:1 says *"In the beginning was the Word, and the Word was with God, and **the Word was God**"* (emphasis added). He is the Word. And the Word He gave me was a loving, quiet, command. It was Jesus' voice. How sweet the sound. I can only describe this revelation by asking if you have ever watched a YouTube video of a child who was born deaf and with the help of a hearing aid, they can hear for the first time? They come alive. The sound is so sweet they cry. Hearing a parent's voice is priceless! That's how I felt when I realized that it was Jesus' voice. Priceless! I still cannot stop saying: Praise you Lord for seeing me, for speaking to Me. Personally. The King of the Universe saw fit to speak to me. To warn me personally. He didn't send an angel to warn me this time. He didn't send the Holy Spirit to warn me this time. He, Himself, warned me. How amazing is that? I knew it was **from** God and now I know it **was** God. It was Jesus' voice.

But there's more. I now understood that I heard the Shepherd's voice and the Bible says that His sheep know Him and hear His voice. *"My sheep listen to my voice; I know them, and they follow me"* John 10:27. I was overwhelmed again. This was a confirmation of my salvation and that I am His. I am His sheep. I hear His voice. I obey His voice. He sees me and He calls me His.

I had a question. I didn't understand why this voice sounded different. If I had not persisted with my question to

RISK TAKER

God in prayer for months and months, I would not have the answer – and the answer was truly a personal revelation.

Ask, Seek, Knock.
*"Ask and it will be given to you;
seek and you will find;
knock and the door will be opened to you.
For everyone who asks receives;
the one who seeks finds;
and to the one who knocks, the door will be opened."*
Matthew 7:7-8

I asked, I sought, and I knocked – and, by God's grace, I found, I received, and the door was opened to me. The same can be true for you.

JAMIE URICK

APPLY IT

What are you asking God for?

_____

_____

_____

_____

_____

_____

_____

_____

APPLY IT

What are you seeking God for?

_____

_____

_____

_____

_____

_____

_____

_____

APPLY IT

What are you knocking for God to open?

_____

_____

_____

_____

_____

_____

_____

_____

_____

RISK TAKER

APPLY IT

Will you persevere? You will not be disappointed.

_____

_____

_____

_____

_____

_____

_____

_____

APPLY IT

When you wake up in the middle of the night do you realize it could be God waking you up? Don't miss it. Use this time to pray, use this time to ask God "What do you have to say to me?"

_____

_____

_____

_____

_____

_____

_____

_____

RISK TAKER

APPLY IT

Read 1 Samuel 3 where the Lord called Samuel while he was lying in bed but he didn't realize it was God. God called him three times before Samuel responded *"Speak, for your servant is listening"* (1 Samuel 3:10). Will you tune your ear to God's voice? Will you say to God in the middle of the night "Speak, for your servant is listening?" He will. The entire Bible is about God's redemptive plan to have His children with Him for eternity in heaven. Walk with Him in the coolness of the day like Adam did, like Eve did, like Enoch did, and be grateful to be woken up in the middle of the night to be with Him. You may think it's your bladder waking you up and maybe it's God – using your bladder.

Today, know that God still speaks.

JAMIE URICK

Are you His? Pray this **Salvation prayer** from your heart and pray it out loud:

"God, I am a sinner, I confess my sins to You and ask for Your forgiveness. I cannot save myself, only You can. I believe that Your Son, Jesus Christ, died on the cross for my sins. Please come into my heart, save my soul, and make me Yours by the power of the Holy Spirit. Thank you for saving me and for answering my prayer. I pray this in Jesus' precious Name, Amen."

CHAPTER FIVE
There's More!

> *"Now to him who is able*
> *to do immeasurably more*
> *than all we ask or imagine,*
> *according to his power that is at work within us,*
> *to him be glory in the church*
> *and in Christ Jesus throughout all generations,*
> *for ever and ever!*
> *Amen."*
> Ephesians 3:20-21

I THOUGHT THE revelations that God saved my life was the pinnacle, then I thought the revelation that the voice I heard was Jesus' voice was the pinnacle and marked the end of the revelations on these three events. Happily, I was wrong. There's more.

One night God woke me up and He brought to my mind these three events: The tractor, the semi truck, and the tie rod

RISK TAKER

breaking. I remembered every detail as if it were yesterday. Then the stories repeated and repeated and repeated. I inquired of the Lord, "Lord, what are You trying to show me? What am I missing?" I almost felt indulgent seeing these stories again and again and again in my mind. Then He said, "You heard the angel warn you. You heard My voice. You felt the prompting of the Holy Spirit." I said, "Yes." But I felt there was more and I didn't understand it. Then, …. He explained to me "You know the difference between an angel speaking, Me speaking, and the Holy Spirit prompting." "You can tell the difference." He went on to say "Most people say they heard from God but you know the difference in Who is speaking. YOU know." I was blown away. Yes! There was no doubt in my mind that the angel said "… you will surely die." I had no doubt that the Holy Spirit prompted me to transfer that money. And, I had no doubt that Jesus was the One who said "wait." and "You hear My voice." But I never put it together before that knowing this means that I know the difference between the three voices. This was another revelation from God that we can hear God and we can know the difference between an angel, the Holy Spirit, and Jesus' voice.

Knowing God's character there is even more that He will reveal to my heart. His revelations are endless.

I share this with you to show you how God speaks so that you can hear His voice. What He did for me, He will do for you. I'm not the focus, He is.

APPLY IT

Now you know that God speaks today. Now you know that He speaks through angels, through the Holy Spirit, and He Himself speaks. Now you know. Will you praise Him?

RISK TAKER

APPLY IT

Will you ask Him to speak to you today? He speaks through creation, through others, through His Word, through dreams and visions. The Bible says *"In the last days, God says, I will pour out my Spirit on all people. Your sons and daughters will prophesy, your young men will see visions, your old men will dream dreams"* Acts 2:17.

_____

_____

_____

_____

_____

_____

APPLY IT

When you are expecting a baby, you prepare a nursery. When God wanted to create man, when He wanted to create you, He prepared an entire world. He created galaxies, stars, earth, animals, plants, and He created seasons and splendor – all in preparation for you. It is all for you to enjoy and to know Him better. You know the person by the gifts they give. God is good. He loves you. He gives you good gifts. He is a good gift.

Jeremiah 29:11 says *"'For I know the plans I have for you,' declares the Lord, 'plans to prosper you and not to harm you, plans to give you hope and a future.'"* What I love about that verse is God doesn't just say it, He doesn't just write it, He declares it. Declares it to whom? He declares it to all of creation, and He declares it to your heart. **Sometimes we are so busy, sometimes our hearts are so troubled that we need someone to shout something to shake us awake**. God is shouting to your heart *"I know the plans I have for you...plans to prosper you and not to harm you, plans to give you hope and a future."*

RISK TAKER

How will you declare that back to God? Declaring it back to God builds your faith, keeps your focus on Him, and ushers in His good plans for you.

_____

_____

_____

Will you receive it?

_____

_____

_____

Will you declare that to your circumstances?

_____

_____

_____

JAMIE URICK

Will you look for the fruit of that verse?

CHAPTER SIX

Conclusion

"He answered, 'Love the Lord your God with all your heart and with all your soul and with all your strength and with all your mind'; and 'love your neighbor as yourself.'"
Luke 10:27

RISK

LOVE IS A risk. I'm taking a risk sharing my faith and sharing how God spoke to me in such personal ways. But He's worth it.

It was a risk for Jesus to die on the cross for all of humanity because some will welcome Him and others will reject Him. But He said "You are worth it."

It was a risk for God to ask me to write this book because I didn't want to. It's that personal. But He's worth it.

RISK TAKER

It was a risk for God to call me to write this book, because not all who are called say "Yes". But you are worth it.

It's a risk for you to believe in Someone you cannot see. But He's worth it.

It's a risk for you to share your faith with someone. But they are worth it.

I am a risk taker. Will you be a risk taker too?

The real risk is in not sharing. The real risk is not obeying God. The real risk is in not responding to His offer of salvation and eternal life with Him.

LOVE

I took a risk by warning my husband about what an angel said because I loved him.

I took the risk of sharing my testimony with you because I love you.

Will you take the risk of trusting Jesus with your eternity because He loves you?

God loved me enough to speak to me through His Word.

God loved you enough to speak to you through His Word.

Will you read His Word which is His love letter to you?

If you don't know where to start, the best Bible study in the world is Bible Study Fellowship. It's free. Check it out at www.bsfinternational.org. There is more in Chapter 8 on where to start your walk with God.

HEAVEN

I am His sheep because I accepted Jesus as my Lord and Savior. Are you His sheep?

If you were to die today and God asks you "Why should I let you into heaven?" What is your response?

Heaven is not for the good, it is for the forgiven.

The only answer is "Jesus paid the price for my sins on the cross and I accepted Him as my Lord and Savior."

THANK YOU

Thank you for reading.

All glory and honor and praise be to God.

Share your testimony and encouragement with me at: Jamie@WarriorHouseLLC.com.

CHAPTER SEVEN
Buyer's Remorse

HAVE YOU EVER purchased something and then wished you hadn't? Maybe it broke soon after you purchased it, or maybe it didn't live up to your expectations. Either way, it was a mistake. Depending on the price you paid it was either a minor disappointment or a major regret. There are many reasons that we experience buyer's remorse.

Did you know that Jesus purchased you? That He suffered and died on the cross, taking on your sins, so that you can be saved? The choice is yours to accept the price He paid, but He paid it nonetheless. He paid for you not with silver or gold but with His blood, with His life (1 Peter 1:18-19) so that you would be free to choose Him.

Do you know what the most amazing thing is? He does not have buyer's remorse. You have not disappointed Him. He is not sorry He bought you. He is not mad at you. He has not abandoned you. You are not an orphan. You have not

RISK TAKER

disqualified yourself. It's not too late to call on Jesus. Your life has purpose. He loves you with an everlasting love. He is stirring your heart right now. Will you receive Him into your heart? Will you love Him back?

CHAPTER EIGHT
The Gospel

THE GOSPEL IS knowing and accepting that Jesus Christ is the Son of God, He was born of a virgin, lived a sinless life, suffered and died on the cross for our sins, He was buried and on the third day He rose again. And *"If you declare with your mouth, 'Jesus is Lord,' and believe in your heart that God raised Him from the dead, you will be saved. For it is with your heart that you believe and are justified, and it is with your mouth that you profess your faith and are saved"* Romans 10:9-10. *"for, Everyone who calls on the name of the Lord, will be saved"* Romans 10:13. *"For God so loved the world that he gave his one and only Son, that whoever believes in him shall not perish but have eternal life"* John 3:16.

When I believe that Jesus is the One who came to redeem sinners (me) from their (my) bondage to sin I am set free from the power and penalty of sin and death.

RISK TAKER

I had lunch with a friend the other day. I asked her "Who is Jesus to you?"

She thought for a bit, looked around, and replied rather hesitantly: "He is the Son of God."

I responded, "Yes, He is. But who is Jesus to **you**?"

She again thought about it and looked around. She again said, "Jesus is the Son of God."

I asked, "Is He your Lord and Savior?"

She replied "Yes."

She may indeed believe that Jesus is her Lord and Savior but I had to be sure. It's too important to not dig deeper.

I explained that you can believe in Jesus Christ and not be saved.

She was surprised. Are you surprised?

I explained that salvation is like a marriage. You can believe in marriage and not be married. You can attend a wedding and unless you are one of the two people taking the marriage vows, you are merely a witness to that ceremony. You can believe in Jesus Christ and not be saved. Christ says the Church is His bride (Ephesians 5:22-23). His Church is not a building it a relationship between God and you. Christ says He is the bridegroom. He is at the head of the church waiting for His bride. A bridegroom is the one who proposes, who prepares a home and a life for His bride. The bride is free to say "Yes" or "No" to the bridegroom's proposal.

Christ's proposal is offered. He is waiting just for you. Will you accept Jesus Christ as your Lord and Savior? Until you say "I do" you are not married to Christ. Like a wedding, it is a one-time event. When you say "I do" you are forever married to Christ.

To believe Jesus is the Son of God and to receive Him into your heart as your Lord and Savior, to say "I do" *out loud* - that is saving faith.

Why out loud? The Bible says *"If you declare with your mouth, 'Jesus is Lord,' and believe in your heart that God raised him from the dead, you will be saved. For it is with your heart that you believe and are justified, and it is with your **mouth** [emphasis added] that you **profess** [emphasis added] your faith and are saved"* Romans 10:9-10.

That means you speak it out loud.

As a confirmation of this, imagine a wedding ceremony where one or both people are silent. They do not say "I do" out loud. What would you think? Some may think they didn't want to get married because they did not consent. No one heard "I do". Others may think they were pressured into it or they had doubts, so they refused to speak and therefore the marriage is not valid. In any case, they leave in the same condition as they came – they are both single. They are not married to each other.

A bride or groom can say all the words, all the right words, but if they don't say "I do" it is not a marriage. They are still single. The same applies to our relationship with Jesus Christ. We can say all the words, all the right words, but if we don't say "I do" to Jesus, to His sacrifice on the cross for our sins, we are not married to Christ, we are not saved.

If you still doubt that you can believe in Jesus as Lord but not be saved, the Bible says *"You believe that there is one God. Good! Even the demons believe that – and shudder"* James 2:19. The demons believe that Jesus is Lord, they have faith, they even shudder, or tremble at His Name, but they are not saved. The demons are going to hell, not heaven. They have faith but they do not have saving faith. Why? They do not have saving faith because they rejected Jesus Christ as Lord of their life.

What does it mean to have a personal relationship with Jesus? What does it mean that Jesus is Lord of your life? With any question we can ask God, and we can look to the

Bible for answers. He gives the answer throughout the Bible, starting in Genesis, in the Garden of Eden. When God made Adam they both loved to walk with each other in the cool of the day. They walked together, they talked together, they sat together, and they enjoyed each other's company. That's what it means to have a personal relationship with Jesus. It is to love to spend time with Him every day. To pray, to talk, to know that He is always with you and that He made you because He loves you. He wants to spend today and all of eternity with you.

The next question was: What does it mean that Jesus is Lord of your life? The answer can also be seen throughout the Bible starting in the Garden of Eden. God made the earth perfect; He made Adam and Eve perfect. Perfect means without sin. God gave man free will. This means we can choose to do good or we can choose to do evil. We each can choose to follow God or choose to follow Satan. There is no third choice. When we choose to follow Jesus, we will not follow perfectly. But when we fail and go to Jesus for forgiveness, He will forgive us. When we say the Salvation Prayer on pages 49 and 72 and when we choose to walk with Jesus that is an example of Jesus being Lord of your life, and having a personal relationship with Him.

If you have confessed with your mouth that Jesus is Lord but doubt your salvation, go to God. Ask Him if you are saved. He will tell you in the most loving way. Salvation is too important to not be sure, it is too important to be deceived in any way. Be sure. God wants you to be sure. The Bible says *"I write these things to you who believe in the name of the Son of God so that you may know that you have eternal life"* 1 John 5:13. Ask Him. You will not wait long for the answer.

When you get married you may not feel any different. But you are indeed married. The same is true with salvation. If you have prayed the salvation prayer you may not feel any different. But you are indeed married to Christ. You are saved. You may not feel any different. That's because the change happens in your spirit, not in your body. Faith is not a feeling. Faith is a decision.

If you don't believe Jesus is real. Ask Him to show you. What do you have to lose?

Bring any unbelief to Jesus and He will answer you. Your eternal destiny is too important to risk, to not know.

Share your testimony at:
Jamie@WarriorHouseLLC.com.

CHAPTER NINE
Where to Start

GOD INVESTED IN you.
Will you invest in Him?

1. **Pray** to the God of the Bible. There is no other God. There is no other way to heaven except through Jesus Christ. John 14:6 *"Jesus answered, 'I am the way and the truth and the life. No one comes to the Father except through me.'"* He is the only way. Some want a different way instead of giving thanks to God that there is a way.

    Nothing is above Him. Nothing is equal to Him. Satan is His enemy. Yes, Satan is real. Satan is our enemy. But not even Satan is equal to God. Satan is a fallen angel.

RISK TAKER

Salvation Prayer. Pray a prayer like this, pray it out loud:

"God, I am a sinner, I confess my sins to You and ask for Your forgiveness. I cannot save myself, only You can. I believe that Your Son, Jesus Christ, died on the cross for my sins. Please come into my heart, save my soul, and make me Yours by the power of the Holy Spirit. Thank you for saving me and for answering my prayer. I pray this in Jesus' precious Name, Amen."

2. **Buy a Bible**. There are many translations. The one I recommend is a New International Version, but you may find another translation you like better. Choose one with a print size that is easy on your eyes. Choose one that has room in the margins to write down notes. Choose one that you will use. If you choose a physical Bible, buy Bible Tabs to mark the beginning of each book in the Bible. There are 66 books in the Bible and having the tabs makes it much easier to find the right book and then the right verse. The 66 books in the Bible are divided into two sections: The Old Testament and the New Testament. A Testament is to testify, it is a statement of belief. The Old Testament was before Jesus walked on the earth. The New Testament Jesus is born and His words, in some translations, are in red letters. There is so much more to share but these are the basics to get started.

If you prefer an app, there are many free Bible apps available. The app my good friend Nancy uses is YouVersion. It contains 2,759 Bible versions in 1,831 languages. Choose the version and language that best serves you. Another great feature of using this app is the ability to read the same Bible verse in different versions seamlessly. The app contains hundreds of Bible plans, devotionals, and podcasts. I recommend new readers to start in the book of John. However, if you decide to start at the beginning, in Genesis, that's great too. Just skip Leviticus for now, you can come back to it later.

3. **How to use a Bible.** Bible verses are divided into three parts. The name of the book, the chapter number, and the verse or verses that are covered. For example: John 3:16. "John" is the name of the book. The "3" is the chapter number, and the "16" is the verse number.

In the beginning of your Bible, you will find the list of the 66 books in the Bible. They will be listed in two ways: Alphabetically, and in order they appear in the Bible. Let's practice by looking up John 3:16. First, find the book of John, then go to the third chapter, and then to the 16th verse. You know you found the right verse if you find: *"For God so loved the world that he gave his one and only Son, that whoever believes in him shall not perish but have eternal life."* Well done!

If the passage to be read was John 3:16-17 that simply means to read two verses. Verses 16 and 17 of John 3.

4. **Find a good church and a good Bible study**. A good church and a good Bible study both have a high view of God and teach that Jesus is Lord and Savior. They teach that Jesus is the only way to God, the only way to heaven. The best Bible study in the world is Bible Study Fellowship (BSF). It is free. It is offered internationally. You may attend in person or online. All are welcome. If you are new to studying the Bible, you are welcome and you will not be intimidated. If you have more knowledge, you are welcome and you will be challenged. It is for everyone, at every age. Make a decision to check out BSF today and to register for the class at www.bsfinternational.org. They meet via zoom September through May at a day and time that is convenient for you or in person at a church near you.

If you have prayed the prayer of Salvation, know that you are saved. Know that you will spend eternity with Jesus Christ in Heaven. You cannot lose your salvation. The strength of the promise is based on God, not on you.

JAMIE URICK

If you doubt that you are saved, bring your doubts to God and He will answer you in the most loving way. This is too important to be deceived. God does not want you to live in fear; God wants you to have assurance of your salvation. Whether you are currently single, married, divorced, or widowed, imagine how would you live, how would you feel, if you were not sure you were married to your spouse? There would not be a firm foundation. There would not be a deep trust level. The same with God. He wants you to have the assurance so that you will have a firm foundation with Him and a deep trust level with Him. I asked God to show me that I was indeed saved because I did not want to be deceived. I did not want to be self-deceived. He was quick to respond and He gave me such sweet assurance and in such a loving way that I have never doubted my saving faith since that day. He wants the same for you. I want the same for you. Walk with Him. Seek Him with all your heart and you will find Him (Jeremiah 29:13). It's ok, God is Good, you can trust in His Good character.

Share your testimony: Jamie@WarriorHouseLLC.com.

Warrior House LLC
P.O. Box 871
Frankfort, Illinois 60423 USA

Jamie@WarriorHouseLLC.com

Look for more books coming out soon by Jamie Urick.